T0145165

MY SPECIAL GIFT

...Reincarnation...

By Cindy L. Conard

Balboa Press books may be ordered through booksellers or by contacting:

Balboa Press
A Division of Hay House
1663 Liberty Drive
Bloomington, IN 47403
www.balboapress.com
1 (877) 407-4847

ISBN: 978-1-5043-9675-2 (sc)
ISBN: 978-1-5043-9676-9 (e)

Library of Congress Control Number: 2018901491

Print information available on the last page.

Balboa Press rev. date: 01/28/2018

BALBOA
PRESS
A DIVISION OF HAY HOUSE

MY SPECIAL GIFT

...Reincarnation...

By Cindy L. Conard

LEARN TO LET GO...

...REMEMBER

This book is dedicated to my niece, Jessica Carter,
without whom the inspiration of this series
would not have come to be.

My name is Isabella and I'm four years old,
I'm too young to know things yet, or
So I have been told.
But stories — I can tell you,
About the places I have been;
And all I have to really do is sit and go
Within.

I have a lot to share with you about
The things I've done;
As we travel back to paradise,
To an island in the sun.
I'd wade and gather shellfish from
The ocean floor,
As I gazed upon the beauty along
The shallow shore.

The palm trees swayed, the wind blew soft,
The sky the brightest blue;
The sand so warm, the flowers bloomed,
It was the perfect view.
A peaceful time, a simple life
Just my husband, child and I;
A fleeting glimpse of memories of a
Time that's passed me by.

I've seen Rome in all its beauty,
Marbled pillars tall and white;
Buildings, gardens, statues — all
Honoring their strength and might.

There is a world of difference here
On the other side of things;
Lack of food and shelter
For the poorer class of beings.

Another group in training
At the dawning of the light;
men young and old in chariots,
On their way to race or fight.

Moving on along now to the
Time of Civil War,
Taking care of farm and home,
And always being sore.
Gone by are times of plenty and
Lazy afternoons;
Along with teas and balls with
merry little tunes.

We work hard to bring in food,
Just to stay alive;
Doing what is necessary
In order to survive.
With husband off fighting, I'm taking
Care of all my own;
When it's finally over
The boys and I ending up alone.

We crossed the prairie in covered wagon
When I was just a child;
Vast wide open spaces and the
Country seemed so wild.
It was all so adventurous until
Winter came at last;
When we settled down to wait it out
And let it pass.

The trip took us longer
Than a year,
Losing friends and family along
The way;
But once we saw the lush green land
We were home and
Here to stay.

Let's cross the ocean now,
To Ireland we go;
We see the mighty cliffs above
And the stormy seas below.
The hills so green, the sky so clear,
The air a misty hue;
A Momma and her boys run
Amidst the morning dew.

With husband gone
And all alone,
It makes a hard and
Lonely life;
But with strength and perseverance,
I get by in spite of strife.

An ancient island long ago,
Using crystals, lasers,
And light;
Where man abused his powers
For healing, learning
And sight.

A civilization so far advanced
Technology was abound;
Where every soul had gifts
And talents
From thoughts and sights
And sound.

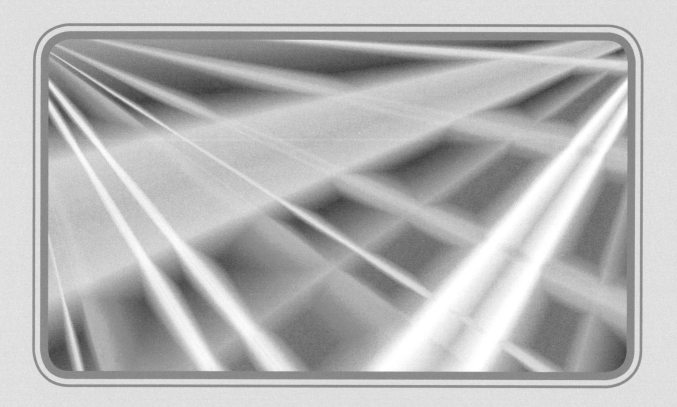

In <u>this</u> time around we can only pray;
That given second chances
    we'll be allowed to stay.

So go to sleep and drift,
    And know that you once knew...

        Go to sleep and dream and
        You'll remember too.

Printed in the United States
By Bookmasters